Deregulation and Energy MLM Email Prospecting Autoresponder Messages for Network Marketing companies offering Electricity or Natural Gas

David Williams

www.DavidWilliamsMLMAuthor.com

Deregulation and Energy MLM Email Prospecting Autoresponder Messages for Network Marketing companies offering Electricity or Natural Gas

ISBN 978-1499574227

Your rights:

Table of Contents

The best way to use this book 1

Your 30 Email Prospecting Messages 9

Post Scripts - PS's 76

Further Resources 79

The best way to use this book

This book contains a professionally written email drip campaign of 30 powerful, engaging and entertaining persuasive email/autoresponder messages focusing on the Energy industry.

These emails are perfect for North American Power, 5Linx, Veridian, CCM Consumer Choice Marketing, Momentis, IGNITE, Ambit, ACN - and any other energy or electricity network marketing company.

If your products include electricity, natural gas or related products, this drip list campaign will engage your prospect and have them calling you.

These autoresponder messages contain humor, personality, and are energy and deregulation related. They are perfect for the person who looking for a REAL residual income.

Each email ends with asking the prospect to call you now as the call to action.

How and Why an autoresponders campaign works:

If you have been in Network Marketing for any length of time, you probably have accumulated a list of prospects and their email addresses. However, many of these prospects have entered the 'witness protection program'. In other words, they never call back or reply to your emails. Most people forget about this list, but there is GOLD in it!

Now, you probably have an email system you pay for that is filled with 'canned' autoresponders about your company, or even some generic versions to send to your list. Sometimes this is part of your 'back-office'.

But, have you read these autoresponders being sent in your name?

They are deadly bad.

Here's why:

They are dry, impersonal and dull.

Let's face it. Most people can't write a note to save their lives, let alone a well-crafted email campaign. Forget learning a skill that will take you years to master – just use these expert messages instead!

That's where this book of powerful 'energy industry' autoresponder messages will come to your aid.

Inside are 30 rock solid emails that focus on your prospects and how they can create a REAL residual income with your company. With engaging humor and playfulness, they will show how YOU and your company and products can help people improve their financial picture, and why energy is the right product for network marketing.

FULL DISCLOSURE – this is a small book – 30 powerful emails. You are not paying for the quantity of words, you are paying for the quality of the message and for getting your phone to ring.

This book contains 30 well-crafted powerfully written emails that are fun and engaging, and that will suggest and reinforce to your prospect that YOU are the answer, the right person to be their sponsor.

Take these email autoresponder messages and enter them into your backoffice or your email program. Start dripping on your list with these professionally written email messages – each crafted to have your prospect motivated to reach out and call YOU as their upline!

How best to use this book

Type each email out, it takes about 3 to 5 minutes for each, and you only need a few at first.

This is why the size of the book is larger than my others.

It's a pretty simple task to type each email out in a word processor. If you were to do one a week, and drip this on your list each week, you will find it is not a burden at all. Of course, it's pretty easy to just type them all out at once. That way you will learn more about the emails you have invested in, and you'll learn more about how to write your own, should you decide to.

Once you have your emails in your word processor you will see that there is a place in each of the emails for your name, your company or networking program name, your prospects name, etc.

There are a few, not many, areas in the emails that you need to change, some if you only have natural gas. Just read through each email and make the changes, it should take you about 5 minutes

Once you have completed personalizing your drip campaign, copy and paste each one into your email autoresponder service or your backoffice, or whatever program or app you use to send your emails. If you don't have any, and you can always send them manually from your own email program like Gmail or Outlook. As you build up your list you can invest in some kind of delivery service like Aweber etc.

One last note, this book has been formatted for easy reading so you can type out each one faster. However you need to format them so that there are only about 40 characters in each line, for example like this:

Hello Prospect-Name,

If you stop to think about it, people are
perceptive creatures by nature - sometimes
way too perceptive - whether consciously
or not. This goes double for those close
to you.

In fact, you are an example. Now what sort
of example do you want to be?

Example 1:

You get up at whatever time you want to
with a happy, smiling face. You turn on
your computer and look at what money your
Company-Name business has deposited in your bank
account. You look out the window from your
home office and think about how good
things are. You give your dog or cat a
friendly scratch at the same time.

Then you take 20 minutes and pay all the
pending monthly bills. And just for the
fun of it, buy a couple of ounces of gold
& silver - for future security.

Finally you decide to take the family out
in the evening for a fun dinner and maybe
a movie.

-END EXAMPLE-

This formatting will get you a much better response.

It makes reading much easier for your prospect, and has been proven to
work much better at keeping someone reading your message right to the
end.

Second, if you have the option to use 'plain text' or HTML with images
etc pick the first, plain text. Plain text out preforms HTML/image
email.

Note that many of the email messages urge your prospect to call you
'now', so remember that when you send these to your list. For that
reason, I really suggest you have your phone number in the contact
section, not a Voice Mail, unless you are part time and unable to take
calls.

If you sign up for my newsletter, you'll get five additional emails
for your autoresponders.

Why is it so important to keep dripping on your list?

Because it works.

There are two reasons why.

1)It is usually between the 7th to the 14th 'connection' or email with
someone that they take action and contact you, if they haven't right
away. This is a proven fact. This works for all types of marketing,
from emailing to person to person. Smart sales people know this, and
some sales people, when meeting personally with a prospect, will ex-
cuse themselves from a meeting to use the washroom, just because the
sheer act of coming back into the room will count as a second 'connec

tion' to the subconscious mind. Amazing! But it's just the way our mind works.

However, many networkers are taught to move on and give up after 3 tries. Or, they send emails out that are so bad, dull, or boring that they are not read, and thus don't count as a connection.

2)The second reason why your drip campaign takes time is because of the 'Hungry Cycle'.

Think of the Hungry Cycle as an up and down scale of need or 'hunger'. When the graph is down, the prospect is 'full' or satisfied with things. His 'hunger demand' is low. Perhaps his boss gave him an inspirational talk about the future, or he received his tax return, or perhaps a loan from a friend or parent. If your email offering to help him earn additional income hits at that moment, he can't 'see' it.

When you feel full, you won't eat, even though you know you need to eat within a few hours, and even though you know your body can store excess calories, you don't eat. If you have just eaten a big turkey dinner, and a friend calls you up and offers to take you to an all-you-can eat Chinese food buffet, the best in the city, right now, you say – 'no'. Thanks, but no thanks.

Same is true for income needs. Even though we need more money, people that get a short term fix will rarely keep seeking to solve their long term needs, until disaster is staring them in the face again. So, what does that mean to you the network marketer? It just means that you keep dripping on your prospects, because sooner or later they will face up to some sort of financial disaster coming their way and become hungry again. They could lose their jobs, hear about layoffs, have a spouse who loses their job, etc., etc.

None of these emails contain any claims that will be against any of the terms and conditions of your program, as they don't make any crazy income promises, or product statements.

FYI: purchasing a professionally written Email campaign is expensive. A recent example I can reveal to you - 19 emails for $12,000, written for an Amway connected person. Don't gasp. That's a fair price for

REAL serious network marketers. Why? Because emails **Do** work. Email is not dead. It's only dead if people send dull, boring or typical canned emails to their prospects.

Remember, you have invested a lot of money in your leads, so don't ever stop selling them until they unsubscribe. Just because they didn't join right away is no reason to stop - EVER! Drip on them weekly or even more often. Drip on them with an email campaign tasked around solving their financial woes until they join or unsubscribe.

Bottom line is this, you ARE going to go through a lot of leads. You'll pay to acquire them one way or another. You will recruit the prospects who are ready, the rest stay on your drip list.

There is money in your list, because eventually the reason your prospect got on this list is going to force them to make a decision.

Who are they going to turn to?

Well, if you have kept in touch with them in a meaningful and personal way, there is a great chance they will turn to you.

But what about those email campaigns you get from your company? They must be good, right? Who wrote those? Professionals, right?

No. Most likely distributor services or some intern admin person. In other words - not a copywriter with an MLM background like I have.

That's why they don't work.

By the way, I took a look at upwards of over 1000 different emails from these so called MLM autoresponder services, thinking some of them must be good. But once I saw them I laughed until I cried. Talk about hard sell, or bad sell.

Who cares about how big the 'home based' industry is, or if your company is 18 years old and solid, or is introducing a new lotion, pill or powder, expanding in South Korea or increasing the PV in your TV?

No one. Don't get me wrong, these are important points for those who are part of your team, but they are features, not benefits. And they are especially not benefits to your prospect.

Now set up your automated drip campaign and watch your gold mine in action. You will find it's nice to know its working for you while you continue to do your primary prospecting. Don't forget, a drip campaign is NOT a replacement for your primary prospecting methods; it is a way to keep working on your list once you have determined a prospect is no longer in your 'hot' pile.

Never give up!

FREE! Five additional Email Autoresponders!!

Sign up for my newsletter and get five more generic email messages!

www.DavidWilliamsMLMAuthor.com

What Example Are You?

Hello Prospect-Name,

If you stop to think about it, people are perceptive creatures by nature - sometimes way too perceptive - whether consciously or not. This goes double for those close to you.

In fact, you are an example. Now what sort of example do you want to be?

Example 1:

You get up at whatever time you want to with a happy, smiling face. You turn on your computer and look at what money your Company-Name business has deposited in your bank account. You look out the window from your home office and think about how good things are. You give your dog or cat a friendly scratch at the same time.

Then you take 20 minutes and pay all the pending monthly bills. And just for the fun of it, buy a couple of ounces of gold & silver - for future security.

Finally you decide to take the family out in the evening for a fun dinner and maybe a movie.

Or Example 2:

You get up at the command of the alarm with a tired, sad face. You ignore your computer to avoid any "pay me" emails. You refuse to think about the bills that are piling up. You look out the window from your kitchen and admit it's time to go to the 9:00 to 5:00 job that you want to quit. You may still give your dog friendly scratch.

Then you go get ready for another day of the same. You do decide that the family deserves a treat tonight and maybe you can swing coming home with a pizza.

And in either example, maybe just maybe, your spouse and or children have gotten up and are you watching you from the doorway.

Which is the example you want and need to be?

What you do with your life is up to only you in the long run after all.

I'll bet you want to live Example 1.

But how?

Look, I know you've been looking at Company-Name and other network marketing companies as well as other options out there.

I know Company-Name is not the only game in town.

For me it's just the one that can move someone into a monthly income as fast as possible.

Why? Because you don't have be a sales person.

You only need to be a 'switch' person.

By that I mean you only need to show people some energy options where they can save money.

Most people like the idea of saving money.

It's not a big deal to them.

You show them the savings and they switch.

Don't think it's that easy, try this sentence out for me:

"Oh, by the way, did you hear about the new laws that were passed on utilities and how so many people are being overcharged but don't realize it? If you have your bill handy, I can take a look at it and see if you are being overcharged."

Was that so hard?

Look, this is how easy it is to make those monthly residual checks.

Call me and I'll hook you up.

Call me now, I'm here.

Best,

Jane

contact info

online movie link

What Did He Say? Earn Pennies?

Hello Prospect-Name,

Have you heard about that guy from Omaha who watched his pennies so well he bought a fleet of jets?

They tell me he's a billionaire - yeah - a billionaire - just from being smart with his money.

Yet he still lives in his small three bedroom house in Omaha, which he bought 50 years ago after he got married. They guy says that he has everything he needs in that little house.

You want to know something else about him, this guy's name is Warren Buffett.

He said that deregulation, the ending of monopolies in energy - would 'lead to the greatest transfer of wealth in our lifetime'.

So I got into the deregulation business.

I show people how to save money each month on their energy bill.

They love it.

I make a little bit of money - pennies and dollars - on each bill.

I can find other folks who want to do the same - and I get a little bit of income based on customers those folks gather.

Yeah, I know pennies.

But that's the genius of Warren Buffett.

Who am I to argue with a billionaire who parlayed pennies into billions?

And, the 'greatest transfer of wealth in our lifetime'?

Yeah.

So if you're ready to follow the path laid out by Warren Buffett, call me and I'll show you how.

The greatest transfer of wealth in our lifetime begins with pennies turning into dollars - your dollars!

Get in on it!

Best,

Jane

contact info

online video

Is Bugsy Siegel Your Mentor?

Hello Prospect-Name,

Honesty time here. Have you ever wondered about the Bad Guys?

Just open the paper and it seems like the Bad Guys have all the money and everything they want.

Have you ever thought maybe, "I should be like them?"

Hey, why not? But before you make the switch, here are some motivating examples.

Bugsy Siegel, founder of the real Las Vegas was a New York Bad Guy who, like a lot of us, decided to head West. Somehow he ended up in the middle of the desert in a no-place town called Las Vegas. But he had his dream board and began to envision a gambling mecca right there. Using dirty money, he put up the famous (or infamous) Flamingo casino.

You know the end of the story: Vegas and Bugsy took off laughing all the way to the bank - until he was killed by other mobsters.

Al Capone delivered what the public wanted during the Prohibition era. He bought booze from Canada legally and sold it in the States illegally. No surprise that he made millions. He finally ended up in jail for tax evasion as everyone whoever watched the Kevin Costner flick 'Untouchables' knows. Soon after getting out of prison he died of Syphilis - which he caught in jail. That was never mentioned in the film.

Look, day dreaming of being a gangster is something everyone has done.

In the movies it might look pretty good.

Just like those network marketing companies that promise to make you rich, give you a yacht, and all you need to do is 'show up and sign up'.

Look, we can dream about it, but it's just not real.

I'll tell you what is real though – a company with a product that requires no big promises because the product is something everyone already uses and requires no selling.

What kind of product is that?

In a word: energy.

Yes, I'll admit the profit on that kind of product is low.

But ask yourself this: What is better?

A high profit on something people are not likely to buy or a low profit on something they are buying already – each and every month!

It's pretty clear that it's better to get paid a few pennies every time someone turns on the lights than when they MIGHT buy that high priced vitamin, or skin care product.

Sure there is more profit in the higher priced product but it's a lot easier to just switch someone from one energy utility to another.

It just makes sense.

And those sense add up to dollars.

And those dollars are real – not 'potential' – no one stops using their lights.

So, can I suggest you forget pie-in-the-sky and start making money?

Join us at Company-Name. Make some steady income that is REAL.

Call me. I'll answer.

Best,

Jane

contact info

online video

Are You a People? Should You Change?

Hello Prospect-Name,

People never change.

We want love and passion.

Not only that, we desire security, purpose, self-satisfaction and of course health. When it comes down to it, we want freedom, fun and often we want financial independence to achieve many of those desires.

We have sought after these same things for all of history. And we will still want these same things a thousand years from now.

It very hard to change people – heck, because we don't want to change.

Everyone wants to lose weight, but at the same time everyone wants to eat. It's hard to change.

I know: I'm one of those.

I know a lot of people see the diet industry as a way to make money.

And I hate it when someone is trying to make money off of my problem and pushing me to change.

I realized that pushing people to change is NOT a way to make money.

That's why I decided to sell electricity.

No one I talk to ever said they don't like to have power in their home or business.

It's not selling, it's switching.

They are not 'changing' themselves – they are just changing their energy provider!

I don't have to 'sell' them on my diet pill, just show them how they can save some money by using our energy plan.

Hey, most people just say 'sure', because we're not asking them do something they don't do now.

People like to light up their home. It won't go out of fashion.

And the kicker?

You can save them money with Company-Name.

It's a no brainer.

People always have liked saving money!

Sound good? Ready to make some STEADY money?

Call me. I'll help you.

Best,

Jane

contact info

online video

Go With God?

Hello Prospect-Name,

Let's forget business for a second, and let me share with you a story about life (and death).

You know, so often someone with a good idea is trying to reach us, we don't see that idea for what it is. Have you heard about the God-fearing man who drowned unhappy with God?

Let me tell you about him. All the TV and radio stations were reporting an alert to everyone to evacuate due to a terrible flood that was 'bigger than Noah's' on the way.

But our God-fearing man did not feel the need to heed the TV. He was sure God would keep him alive.

Soon the rain started and there was water everywhere, people were leaving their homes - except one.

Now a National Guard jeep drove by and a soldier asked this man to get in, so he could be taken to safe place to wait out the flood.

"No," he said, "God will send me any help I may need."

The rain continued until it was up to this guy's porch. A small National Guard boat came and the Guardsmen asked, "Would you like to get in and we'll take you to a safer place?" The man answered, "No, my Lord will provide."

Now the rains kept falling - by this time the man was sitting up on his roof, looking at the dark clouds.

Right then, a National Guard helicopter flew down and the aircrew shouted, "Climb on the ladder and we'll save you."

The man answered again, "No, my God will save me."

Well, you have guessed the end of the story. The poor guy drowned.

However he went to heaven, where it was dry.

Dry or not, he wasn't a happy camper. When he saw God he said, "Father, I don't understand. Why didn't you send any help?"

"What?" God replied. "I sent you a warning, a jeep, a boat and a helicopter – what more did you want?"

Now I'll bet you are not facing a flood right now, but if you're drowning – drowning in debt – then why not take this outstretched hand full of money we're offering?

'What!?"

"What's that you say, what money?"

The money you are leaving on the table from all of the deregulation that the Feds did twenty years ago.

Warren 'The Boss' Buffett said deregulation would mean a jackpot was coming your way – if you stand in the way to collect it!

Now Warren's not God by any stretch, but he knows a thing or two more than you and I know about money – so don't wait any longer – call me now to see how fast you can collect on it.

Call me and I'll fill you in.

Best,

Jane

contact info

online video

News about Spiderman… READ NOW!

Hello Prospect-Name,

Spiderman was one of my fav superheroes.

He was really on his own – not liked by the cops or by the establishment and certainly not liked by the crooks.

It reminds me of networking.

Network marketing outperforms the regular old time dinosaur business model.

The mass media don't like us either – because we never buy ad space.

Is your 'Spidey Sense' tingling? It should be because that's why you only read negative articles in the press about networking and MLM.

As far as others are concerned, deregulation is something that only Wall Street is concerned about – it has nothing to do with the average Joe or Jane.

But it does – because Company-Name has combined deregulation with networking – meaning the average person can take advantage of it too.

Any of us average folks can make above average incomes by offering deregulated products to anyone or any business.

We can offer them the same energy – but for less!

And we can earn a profit from it too!

Come on – use that Spidey Sense and pick up the phone and call me. I'm right here and ready to show you how you can be a 'player' in dereg too!

Best,

Jane

contact info

online video

Going to (with) the Dogs

Hello Prospect-Name,

What do you think about dogs?

Some people say they are nicer companions than people.

But chewing on your shoes - well - I never had that problem with my goldfish.

I always heard that dogs were warm, loyal, but kind of well, simple?

Turns out I was wrong (again!) Dogs are actually linear thinkers.

Like us, dogs take their time to get what they want. And it turns out that they are stubborn about it too.

I read that they even set goals and go for them! Horse patootie I thought... until the following day.

I was sitting on my patio enjoying my work-at-home lifestyle.

From where I was, I could see over to my neighbor's house. In an open patio, he had his toolbox that he uses about the house just sitting on a table. On the top of the toolbox was an old rag.

Now this neighbor has a huge mutt. This mutt was eyeing the rag. (My neighbor was out at the moment.)

The dog first tried to go up on hind legs to reach his goal.

Turned out - like many of our goals - it was too high.

He then tried jumping.

No, not working.

He even tried biting into the cabinet, but to no avail.

By this time I couldn't look away.

He laid down on the grass and stared his goal. Then I swear I saw an 'idea lightbulb' go off above his head.

He tore off to the back of his house.

When he returned he had a long cane in his mouth – used my neighbor's mother-in-law's!

Long story short. The mutt got up on his hind-legs and used the cane to wiggle the rag down to his waiting mouth.

The cane was a little worse for wear but still – he achieved his goal.

Amazing.

Remember that light bulb that went off as Fido got the idea on how to reach his goal?

Well, if you were in Company-Name, you would have earned some money.

That's because we get paid each time someone turns on the lights… Now that's a good idea.

Fido is not alone.

I'll bet you have a goal too.

And it's to earn a residual income. Now that's a fancy term for getting money long after you did some work.

If you showed me how to save money on my energy bill each month, YOU would actual earn a part of what I pay the utility company.

Nice.

And those little bits add up each month…they call that residual income. I call it better than a pension!

If you don't have a pension or just plain want some residual income – call me – I can show you how to make that happen.

If dogs can achieve their goals so can we!

Best,

Jane

contact info

online video

PS. My neighbor's dog hates the dark so I suggested they leave the light on all night. Bingo my pension just went up!

I Don't Have the Crabs, Stop Saying I do!

Hello Prospect-Name,

I was told this story from one of the members of my Company-Name network.

I just have to share it with you.

This guy was in a small fishing town on the Northeastern coast.

With the intent of buying some crab for dinner, he came across a seasoned fisherman who was selling these little critters.

The vendor looked like something out of a Hemingway novel. Sixty plus, missing some teeth, slightly bowlegged, sun baked like a Brazil nut. Of course complete with an oversized, worn, slouch hat.

The crabs were the local variety. They were lounging peacefully around the bottom of a huge Coleman - doing whatever crabs do before they are bought, boiled and eaten. (With drawn butter and garlic - perfect!)

The two men started to shoot the bull, hopefully to lead to a successful business transaction. At one point, the fisherman smiled and said, "I'll bet you didn't know that these here crabs can teach us a lot about human nature?"

"What do you mean?"

Before I give you the answer, I ask you to think about your situation. Are the people around you dragging you down with negative feedback about what you want to do? Especially in regard to network marketing?

The crabs have the answer for you. Read on.

The old salt tore a strip off a rag and smeared it with some goo that crabs obviously considered a delicacy. The rag was dipped in the water and the old man held the other end. "Watch."

It didn't take long until one of the crabs went for the goo. It started to climb up the rag for more. Almost immediately the others rose up, pulled the intrepid crab down and tried to take its place – yet the same thing happened to each subsequent crab.

"There's your lesson. Most people will go out of their way to stop others from getting ahead."

It's the same in network marketing.

Everyone tells you they are in it for the residual income – yet they sell products that people rarely buy or are too expensive to be purchased each month.

Sure, in theory everyone wants their monthly skin care cream or vitamin juice – but once there is a little financial problem at home they stop buying.

Autoship cancelled

Let's face it, if you are financially challenged you just pay what you must.

Like your utility bills.

Let me say it again:

"Like Your Utility Bills."

Yes, you see it.

You see the genius here…

COMPANY-NAME is a utility company.

Your customers will pay their bills in good times or bad.

And the good thing is you SAVE your customers money when you help them switch to Company-Name.

Yet the 'crabs' pitching the 'big deal' MLM's keep hyping overpriced autoship plans and expensive products.

Come one, residual income comes from what people pay residually – utility payments.

So say no to the crab mentality trying to keep you down in their barrel.

Call me and we can get you started down the REAL residual path.

Best,

Jane

contact info

online movie link

What Makes an Adventurer a Success?

Hello Prospect-Name,

The pilot decides to soar above others. First he completes ground school. Does flight time with an instructor. Completes solo time. Takes the final flight and oral exams. License in hand, the pilot puts the key in the airplane's ignition, clears with the control tower. And voilà, the pilot takes to the sky free and happy.

The diver decides to see what very few others will ever see. He practices in a swimming pool. Takes swimming tests in the open water. Learns how the diving equipment works. Does practice and final certification dives with an instructor. License in hand, the diver checks the respirator and other equipment, and back flips off a dive boat. And voilà, the diver takes to the depths free and happy.

The MLM entrepreneur decides to get ahead. The entrepreneur does research and joins the best company available. Learns the ropes. Devotes some time to building the business. Starts to see extra income coming in. And voilà, income in hand, the entrepreneur goes into the future free and happy.

It's probably not a hard guess to know which adventurer you are ready to be. (Maybe all three, is up to you after all.)

So that next step is the research and training.

Lucky for us it does not have to be hard.

If this makes sense to you have passed the first test:

Every month people pay for their utilities – like energy.

If someone could offer them the same service for a lower price they'd say 'sure'.

After all, if it's the same you might as well pay the lowest price you can.

And if you can earn a tiny percentage of their new, lower bill, as a reward for bringing that new customer to their new provider – Company-Name – than everyone is happy.

It's called residual income – but I call it an entrepreneurial adventure.

So, if you want a voilà in your life, Company-Name is your license to be free and happy when you decide to take it.

So why not take it now?

Call me. I will answer and help you on your new adventure.

Best,

Jane

contact info

online movie link

Warren Buffett About Autoship

Hello Prospect-Name,

Did you hear about the oil prospector in heaven?

Warren Buffett retold this story that you just must read…

Here is the story of the oil prospector who met Saint Peter at gates of Heaven.

When told of his occupation, Saint Peter remarked, "Oh, I'm terribly sorry. While you do have the right to get into heaven, we've a terrible challenge. Look at that room over there. That's the cloud where we put the oil prospectors who are waiting to get into heaven. And it's filled – we haven't even got room for even one more."

The oil prospector thought for a minute and said, "Would you mind if I spoke to them…for just a second?"

"There's no harm with that," said Saint Pete.

So the old-timer cupped his hands and yelled out, "Oil discovered in Hades!" Instantly, the heavenly prospectors twisted the lock open and flew off, flapping their angel wings as hard as they could aiming for 'the other place'.

"You know, that's a pretty smart stunt," St. Pete said. "Move in. The place is yours. There's plenty of room."

The old prospector thought to himself and said, "I better not…I think I'll follow them down - you never know there could be some truth to that rumor after all."

You see, even people who make up rumors fall for them.

Like the one that you can only make residual cash in network marketing if you sell a product with a monthly autoship.

Yet most people who are in autoship programs know how hard it is to keep people on them.

Why? Because in order to get paid you must be on autoship.

And if there are people in your downline that are not working that hard, or find that life is getting too busy for them to work their business, well, autoships are the first to go.

Look, people come and go in all network marketing companies.

Even Company-Name.

But there is a big difference.

Even when a distributor becomes passive and stops working the business, there is no autoship to cancel with Company-Name.

Yet there are still residuals.

Why?

Because our product is energy.

And no matter what, no one stops using their lights.

That means the residuals keep flowing.

This means you get paid each month.

And guess what?

Since I started talking to other networkers about Company-Name - telling them there's no autoship - guess what?

They love it and jump in.

Come on, give me a call, the lights are on and I'm home!

Best,

Jane

contact info

online movie link

Tweet or Dollars? Your Choice.

Hello Prospect-Name,

It is no secret that politicians use Twitter tweets to get elected. They tweet to get their lies – sorry – promises out to us.

Now, if you can't find a job, here is what you can do:

Tweet your congressmen. Tweet your state senators. If Obama cares, tweet him. You might want to tweet Michelle for good measure too.

Here are some examples to get you started.

@... Voted for you. I Need financial bailout. Send loan?

@... Voted for you. My savings are sick. Send advice for cure?

@... Voted for you. Have huge financial deficit. Approve credit?

Nothing yet? That's very hard to believe but don't give up.

Time for Round 2.

@...Don't care about voters? Shame on U. Sending 1000 tweets to your followers. Enjoy!

And hey, there is free software you can use to automatically send preprogrammed tweets at any time any day.

There you have it. Of course you will never have to go to Round 3. We all know that your elected officials care about you as a constituent. And we know that they will bend over backward to help you in any way they can after getting your initial tweet.

Of course, if by some chance that does not bring you financial help, I have an alternate.

You guessed it, its Company-Name. Why? Because it works, it makes sense, and it – unlike a politician it is dependable.

How can network marketing be any more dependable than a politician you ask?

Well, good question.

The answer is this: each dollar you earn in Company-Name is based on people using their electricity.

You don't have to 'hope' they'll continue to use electricity each morning. It's not a habit they'll stop.

You can take our dependence on energy to the bank - and with the move from gas powered cars to electric cars - your bank account's future looks a lot brighter - if you make the decision to call me and get on the deregulation bandwagon.

Look, don't worry 'how' - that's my job to show you the ropes.

Call me now and I'll start showing you…

Or - you could just tweet Washington for help…

Best,

Jane

contact info

online movie link

The Richest Man in Babylon

Hello Prospect-Name,

The book The Richest Man in Babylon has been around for decades. It always has been, and still is, a Bible on how to get ahead and stay there.

Babylon is a short book about a man seeking to find financial success. So this fellow, a bit like you or I, finds and questions the Richest Man there in what was then the world's richest city.

Turns out that the richest man in Babylon also started out poor and continually kept at his dreams until he achieved success.

Now this Babylonian Warren Buffett gives advice on several topics. In one talk he says to put away 10% of anything you earn.

The seeker asks why so little. Why? Because, he says, if you only keep 10%, you will not miss it in your day-to-day financials. And that little amount will keep growing without you worrying about it. If you try to save more, you will probably raid the larder later on – and mess up everything you've started.

It was really the Richest Man in Babylon that convinced me that Company-Name was the way to go.

Sure, the monthly income starts slow. But each month, more and more residuals show up in our bank account.

That's because the flow is dependable.

And it adds up each month.

And it continues.

Because it's based on the use of energy – something that is never going to go out of style.

Start switching folks to Company-Name's energy and your bank account will grow too.

But over time the income continues. Let you money grow without worrying. Then you can sit back and become the richest man of your town.

Company-Name is your ticket to sustained income.

Call me now and I'll get you started.

Best,

Jane

contact info

online movie link

Just Like Good Ole' Dad

Hello Jane,

This is a story my friend Mark tells. Let me know if it rings a bell in your life:

When I was growing up, my father was a typical example of how the middle class work ethic well...worked.

Dad worked for an auto-part manufacturer. His daily task was to load the plastic wrapped cases of left-fenders onto a wooden pallet. The wrapped fenders were then shipped to parts stores. I went to the factory a couple of times just to watch him when I was just a little kid.

My father's day seldom changed. He got up at the crack of dawn, dressed and packed the same lunch each day: tomato and cheese sandwiches and a carton of milk.

It took 45 minutes for him to get to work. He was on that machine until 5:00. When he came home, we'd eat - Mom always had supper on the table. After dinner, he'd ask me what I learned in school, and then lay down on the couch and watch the news. He would eventually fall asleep right there until the test pattern came on, when he's wake up to go to bed.

That was my Dad's life from Monday to Friday, and often on weekends too when overtime came along.

Dad left us 30 years ago and with him so did the 40-year job that he had.

But times change.

Now Mark can't get one of those jobs that last for 40 years.

But Mark can create an income for himself and his family that will last 40 years - or more!

How? By taking advantage of deregulation.

That and the fact that everyone will never stop using electricity.

All Mark has to do is join us here at Company-Name and help people save money.

He doesn't have convince anyone that energy is a good thing or that they need it.

He just shows them how to save money each month on their utility bills, and he gets a small piece of the action.

A small piece of the biggest thing since the Internet – the energy market.

(You can live without the internet, but you can't live without energy!)

So call me now and I'll help you on the path to getting a 40-year-income plan!

Best,

Jane

contact info

online movie link

Mark Twain's Forgotten Quote About Network Marketing

Hello Prospect-Name,

I never studied history, but as far as I know Mark Twain never joined any networking marketing company.

Sad as that is, (he was often broke and could have used the money), he sure was a wise observer of human nature.

Those of you who have read anything written by him know he could really highlight the lighter side of our dreams and fears.

I often read Twain for his down-home humor and for his inspiration.

As network marketing is really a great metaphor for life, it is no surprise that much of what Twain said could have come straight out of an MLM training course:

"Don't go around saying the world owes you a living. The world owes you nothing. It was here first."

"The lack of money is the root of all evil."

"It's not the size of the dog in the fight, it's the size of the fight in the dog."

"A person with a new idea is a crank until the idea succeeds."

It's that last one that really is important.

There is a new idea out there for networkers.

That you can make money by offering something boring.

You see? You re-act that boring is a crank idea.

But hear me out.

You see, networkers are always trying to trying to sell something 'new', exciting and different – you know – the latest and greatest new wrinkle cream or vitamin or juice.

It seems that 90% of networkers would rather offer a 'bright shiny object' than just make consistent 'boring' money.

I don't know about you, but I got into business because I needed to make money and because I didn't want to sell stuff.

That's why I chose to offer energy.

I don't need to 'sell it' because everyone knows what it is.

Yeah it's boring – yeah it's not new.

But it's easy to find customers because it is boring – they already are SOLD on using it!

I show them that they can save some money and they say 'sure, why not'.

So that makes you money.

The biggest challenge for old-school network marketing companies is to keep their distributors buying their high-priced products.

See why it's much smarter to offer a lower-priced energy that people want anyway?

And I think you are that smart.

Call me now and prove it to yourself.

As Twain also said:

"The secret of getting ahead is getting started."

So give me a call now, and I'll get you started.

Call me, I'm here…

Best,

Jane

contact info

online movie link

Are You Smarter Than My 6th Grader?

Hello Prospect-Name,

I know you're still making a decision to join me here with Company-Name so in the mean time I thought we could have a little fun with this little quiz… see if you recognize any of these names...

(Fun is good, in case you have forgotten that!)

It's a direct sales quiz:

In the 1860's some traveling salesmen trained sales organizations to market their products more widely. Two notable names were Henry Heinz and Asa Chandler. (Ok, you can guess Heinz pretty easily, but Chandler was behind Coke!)

Next came companies that allowed their salespeople to be their own boss. One was the California Perfume Company (1890). Know them? The company changed its name to Avon in 1937.

In 1905 the Fuller Brush Company started paying its dealers by commission only. I still remember them coming to our house, and my Mother buying from the nice guy who visited.

In 1931 Frank Stanley Beveridge, a former executive of Fuller formed Stanley Home Products. Here some dealers started doing in-home presentations for little groups. Significance? The 'party plan' was born.

Did you know who trained Mary Kay Ash (Mary Kay Cosmetics) Brownie Wise (Tupperware) and Mary Crowley (Home Interiors)? They all were trained by Fuller.

In 1934 Carl Rehnborg started the California Vitamin Corporation. The name was changed to Nutrilite in 1339. In 1945 Nutrilite created the first known MLM compensation and dealer systems. Guess who owns them now? - Yes, Amway.

Now that quiz was from the old days…

150 years and growing strong.

What's new?

The fact that networking and deregulation have embraced each other.

How does the idea of making money on commercial energy sound to you?

On home energy?

It's the most amazing thing to hit networking because it means you don't have to 'sell' or convince - like they did in the days of Nutri-lite.

No, just show folks savings and get paid each month on their energy usage.

Brilliant.

It's time for you to get into the brilliant idea too.

No need to wait 150 years - I'm here now to get you started in Company-Name.

Best,

Jane

contact info

online movie link

You Want to Get in on Michael Jackson's Act?   There Are Royalties Enough for All…

Hello Prospect-Name,

Did you know Michael Jackson's singing makes more money today than when he was alive?

According to Clash Magazine, the estate of Michael Jackson has made a huge boost in sales - an increase by 70% - after his death.

Now these royalties - money paid out long after Michael recorded his songs - are paid monthly.

His estate is doing very well.

Every month the estate can sing all the way to the bank.

That's what I like about monthly income - especially the kind that keeps going.

You see, one day those royalties to Michael's estate will start to decline.

Why?

Because he's dead.

People's taste change with the times.

It's a fact.

Ask the estate of Al Jolson.

But there are things that people buy each month, no matter what.

Like energy.

That is not something that goes out of style like Glenn Miller.

Who? Well, he was big in the 30's and 40's but not so much anymore.

That's my point.

That's what Company-Name does.

We offer energy.

Something that people and businesses pay for each month.

And our reps - you and I - get paid on that energy consumption each month.

No worries about people changing their taste, or cancelling their 'autoship'.

That's why there is so much money to be made here - and can it be yours - every month.

If you are not planning a singing career, than call me - and I'll show you how to make a recurring monthly income that is steady and dependable.

Best,

Jane

contact info

online video

George Burns – Network Marketing Trainer?

Hello Prospect-Name,

Read what George said:

Don't stay in bed, unless you can make money in bed.

Now, I'm not advocating staying in bed all day – but I like the idea of being paid while I'm there.

It was why I joined my first MLM company.

Yeah, I bought it hook, line and sinker.

'Just do what you have to do for one year, and you can do what you want to do for the rest of your life.'

Sure.

Tried that and found out no one else wanted to buy these very expensive bottles of vitamins – I still have a cupboard full of them.

Nothing wrong with them – I liked them and used them – but the monthly cost was too high – they called it 'autoship' meaning you get them without thinking.

Well, people would get the bill, $129 per month for vitamins, and they'd start thinking 'TOO EXPENSIVE!'

And then they would cancel.

The only people who stayed on autoship were those who had to in order to get paid.

And once their monthly income dipped below $129, they cancelled too.

My upline told me it was my fault, I did not 'sell' the high value of these little pills enough.

I told him I was no salesman when I joined. He said, "We don't sell, we share."

For crying out loud, now his tune has changed.

So, I forgot about MLM for a while, and just sat at home watching late night infomercials.

My bills were piling up and I needed to make money.

It was then that a friend of mine offered to look at my energy bill and see if he could find out if he could save me some money each month.

"Hey, sure," I said.

"Save me money? Please do."

He looked and said that if I switched to Company-Name I could save a bit each month.

Why not, it was time to save some money.

But I was interested in how he came about offering energy savings.

How did he get into that business? This was a guy who was a computer nerd.

He said it was network marketing, that they sold energy.

Right away a light came on!

This guy was no salesmen – he was the complete geek – no offence to you geeks.

And the best part, he said, was he got paid each month on all of the energy he sold, and that of his downline.

I asked him about 'autoships'?

He did not even know what I was talking about.

"Perfect," I said, and went to one of their meetings to get started.

If you are sick of autoships - and ready to make money each month - call me - and I'll show you how you can be making money in your bed!

Best,

Jane

contact info

online video

Well Spike My Tires and Call Me a Dog…

Hello Prospect-Name,

There are a lot of dogs named Spike but there was also a British comedian named Spike.

Spike Milligan.

He was part of the 'goon' squad with Peter Sellers.

I bring up his name because I think his attitude about money is something we all believe, but don't want to admit to:

"All I ask is the chance to prove that money can't make me happy."

I laughed when I first read that line, but realized later that it's kind of true.

All my life people told me I won't be happy if I was rich, 'so quite looking at stuff' and be thankful you have a job to go to each day'.

Yeah, each day.

Each day.

Well, all I knew was that I was NOT happy doing that job.

I wanted to test out Spike's thesis – will I be happy with money?

I wanted to try it on for size!

So I kept reading ads online about making a gazillion dollars from home in a week without working. Some of the ads said I didn't even have to get dressed – I could make all that cash in my underwear sitting in my kitchen.

Now, I don't know about you, but at our house we have a rule against sitting in the kitchen in just our underwear. So I passed on that one.

Finally, I heard about something that was different.

It did not promise a mega-cash payout. In fact, it was about making a steady flow of money each month, and getting it month after month…would I like to know more?

Sure would - so I clicked on the ad and provided my email address.

Turned out to be about offering small business and regular people (like me) the opportunity to save each month on their energy bill.

If I could do that, the energy company would pay me a commission on whatever those new customers used. Each month, forever!

Not only that. I could build a team and offer this opportunity to others through networking and I'd get a commission on new customers that my team found.

The lights were on in my head, and I was IN!

If you like the idea of offering an opportunity to get a monthly income based on energy - call me now and I'll show you how.

It works!

Best,

Jane

contact info

online video

I'm Such a Snob - Are You Too?

Hello Prospect-Name,

Someone told me I had the wrong attitude about money.

I was one of those who believed 'money doesn't make you happy', but at the same time I was always trying different ideas to make money.

Something was wrong. I was never happy just sitting at home in front of the TV - I was always looking at the computer trying to figure out just how to make some extra cash.

Then a smart friend of mine emailed me this:

It's a kind of spiritual snobbery that makes people think they can be happy without money.

Albert Camus

I had a long, deep think about this.

After careful consideration, contemplation and many sleepless nights, I had to agree. I was guilty of being a spiritual snob.

I preached that happiness came without money.

Yet there I was, without money and unhappy.

What was going on with my life?

Talk about conflicted!

So I wrote my friend back to say she was right.

"What should I do now?"

She said simple: Decide once and for all if you want money or not? Because even if you are not happy, it's much easier to be unhappy and have money.

And having money did eliminate my worries about bills, payments, debts, mortgages and taxes.

I said, "OK, I want money - but how?"

She told what she was doing - helping people save money on their energy bills.

She said I could learn how to do that too.

I told her I knew nothing about energy or accounting. I knew nothing about saving money either!

She calmed me down and met up with me.

She said 'Repeat after me:

Oh, by the way, did you hear about the new laws that were passed on utilities and how so many people are being overcharged but don't realize it? If you have your bill handy, I can take a look at it and see if you are being overcharged.

So I repeated it.

She said that is all I had to do.

 "Once I get someone's energy bill, I show them an option to save money with a different provider - one that I personally use and recommend - that will save them money each month."

No one ever regretted saving money.

And the best part is she gets a commission based on the customers' energy usage - just for getting a new person who likes saving money!

"Not bad," I said, "But you must have to get a lot of customers to afford that Lexus you're driving? How many customers do you have?'

She laughed and said, "I only have about 63, but I have found so many people, like you, to do the same. I show them what I showed you, and they find 50 or 60 too. And the energy company pays me a commission on those as well. It really adds up!"

Wow.

That ruled.

And the best part is that there is no selling, no one needs to be 'sold' on saving money.

And they don't stop using energy later. These days' people leave the lights on even when they're not at home!

I signed up.

Look. If you're ready to end being a 'lack of money' snob – call me – I'll show you how you can do what I do and really change your life.

This works!

Best,

Jane

contact info

online video

How to Beat Bill Gates

Hello Prospect-Name,

Bill Gates was speaking about people – and what Microsoft has to do to them to get sales:

We've got to put a lot of money into changing behavior.

It's the biggest part of their message – to change our behavior so we'll buy their products.

Why? Because changing someone's behavior is not easy.

Even when we want to change, it's not easy.

That's the reason things are so expensive – because of the marketing costs associated with getting people to do something different – to change – to buy something they never bought before or don't think they need.

That is what we call 'hard sales' or 'hard selling'.

It's painful to be on either end of that sale. No one likes their behavior challenged.

That's the big challenge of networking.

Getting people to change their behavior. Paying more for vitamins or skin care products and having them shipped in monthly.

No matter what you say, people resist, "Hey, I can get it cheaper right at the store, and there's no shipping charges."

"Oh, but our product is the BEST."

But everyone says that…

For me, I think it's just better to not challenge people's behavior and offer them what they already want and need.

That's the security of success for Company-Name.

We don't try to change anyone's behavior.

In fact, we are glad they'll continue to use energy…that behavior is not going to change.

Gee, did I forget to tell you we offer energy? You know, like electricity?

Using it is a habit no one will change. Watching TV, charging up the iPad, running the refrigerator, and lately, plugging in the eCar!

Yes sir, using energy is a behavior that needs no explanation or will it go out of style.

We offer the same energy for a lower price, and Company-Name pays us a commission.

Finally, 'no selling'!

Are you ready to stop trying to change peoples' minds and starting making money?

Call me, call me now and I'll get you going,

Best,

Jane

contact info

online video

Woody Allen's Strange Views of Wealth...

Hello Prospect-Name,

I'm not a Woody Allen fan, but then again I'm not a fan of poverty.

So it's not often I agree with this wealthy guy except for his off-handed remark about poverty:

Money is better than poverty, if only for financial reasons.

Woody Allen

Woody thought he was being funny, but poverty is pretty serious.

Being broke is a serious matter.

And many people who are broke are seeking ways to earn cash – like network marketing – but the problem is the huge investment in products.

That's why I chose to market electricity.

Yes, it's a network marketing company – but look – you don't have to buy products to resell – and you don't have to buy products just to qualify on 'autoship'.

No, you just offer energy at better rates than people are already paying – and Company-Name will pay you every month just for helping people save money.

Genius – much smarter than any of Woody's movies.

So, if you don't have a big pile of cash to buy into some network marketing companies 'positioning' scheme – get involved with Company-Name today.

It pays to sell energy – it really pays.

Best,

Jane

contact info

online video

Will You Live Past 4PM Today?

Hi Prospect-Name,

A few old-timers will remember the name of Henny Youngman, but the rest of us won't know who the heck he was.

Well, I'll let you in on it – he was one of these old vaudeville performers who made the transition from stage to TV.

A bit of a comic, and he played the violin too.

One of his most famous lines was...

"Take my wife, please."

I know, pretty lame.

But what he said about money was pretty sound. Let me know if you can relate:

I've got all the money I'll ever need, if I die by four o'clock.

That's his main worry – will my life out last my savings or income?

It's not a joke either.

At least not for me.

I see the writing on the wall, we middle class types are being squeezed out by the government on one hand and big business on the other.

The government taxes our paychecks so much it's about as funny as a Henny Youngman joke.

And big business – well they are moving all the jobs to Mexico or further.

Either way we are on our own.

The only option is our own business.

How about this? Offer a product everyone needs, wants, and is willing to pay for – and uses each day?

And add in you can offer that product and saving your customers money too?

That's a formula to make money.

What is it?

It's getting into the energy game.

It's offering energy at a discount – at a lower rate than people are paying for now and collecting a nice monthly reward from the energy company.

Sound completed? Not at all.

Free training provided, and I'll be with you all the way.

So, if this makes sense to you, call me.

"How would you like to get paid every time someone turns on their lights?"

If a light bulb just went on in your head you could be making money!

Call me now and I'll get you started,

Best,

Jane

contact info

online video

How to Win Big at Monopoly - There Are New Rules

Hi Prospect-Name,

Remember monopolies? When one company controlled all the long distance, electricity or the steel manufacturing?

Well they were great if you were the owner - but not if you had to buy a bit for your drilling rig from a monopoly.

Howard Hughes ran an oil drilling tool manufacturing company what was forever being accused of being a monopoly - but this was how he described it:

We don't have a monopoly. Anyone who wants to dig a well without a Hughes bit can always use a pick and shovel.

So, if you did not want his drilling bit - roll up your sleeves dig a hole by hand.

That's like saying if you don't like our electricity, buy a candle.

And that's the way it was until deregulation a few years ago.

That's right - but those monopolies were outlawed by Congress.

It means we have competition now - and that means lower prices.

Look, I'm not writing to save you money - sure you can - but more importantly I'll looking for someone to work with me in helping a whole mess of people to save money on their electricity bills.

It's a great deal - it's not about selling energy - everyone knows they need energy. It's just about showing them where they can get a better deal on it.

And the company pays us a commission on every dollar spent.

Its win-win - the customer saves money and you and I make money.

I'd love to show you how. Call me now and I can.

Best,

Jane

contact info

online video

The Star Trek Way to Wealth

Hi Prospect-Name,

Remember James Kirk? Who over-acted boldly where no man went before?

Well Kirk said a lot of things.

Thinks like, "Beam me up Scotty." It became a catchphrase.

But something he said long after he retired as an Admiral with Star-fleet stuck with me, see if it makes sense to you:

If saving money is wrong, I don't want to be right! - William Shatner

James Kirk aside, who could disagree with that?

And that's the point behind the success of Company-Name.

You see, we save people money each month on their energy bills.

It's something we can all agree about – we want cheaper energy.

Now I know you've been looking at various network marketing companies.

I know that many pitch their fantastic products.

I buy a few from friends who sell them too.

They tell me it would be easier if I just signed an autoship pledge – the company would charge my credit card and add shipping and handling and send the products straight to my house.

But you know what? I don't want to do that. Sometimes I'm not at home to collect them. Sometimes I don't finish last month's.

I hate being tied down.

Sure it's better for them – but I like my independence.

I'm already dependent on energy.

I admit it.

Why fight it?

I can't fire my photon torpedoes without energy - or watch TV.

I need to pay for energy each month.

And that's the point.

Wouldn't you rather offer something to someone that they are dependent on, and will buy each month AND where they will save money because you showed them how?

You can depend that people will pay their energy bill - but you can't depend that their autoship won't be canceled.

Call me now and I'll show you how to get started, how to build up an energy customer base, how to find customers the EASY way, and how to recruit a team of others that will do the same.

Come on, call me.

Best,

Jane

contact info

online video

How to Buy Assets With Nothing Down

Hi Prospect-Name,

This is one of my favorite quotes from Robert Kiyosaki. It's about assets.

The rich buy assets. The poor only have expenses. The middle class buys liabilities they think are assets.

If you are broke, chances are you are always seeking a way to get back on your feet making money again.

Now, you can have a 'rich' mindset and be broke.

For example if you can acquire assets of value with 'nothing down,' like houses for example, you can follow Kiyosaki's advice and begin to re-build your asset portfolio.

Now for me, real estate is iffy. Perhaps it's a good idea in some places in the US, or in the word for that matter – where you can do well by buying with nothing down. Many do.

But I can tell you an easier way.

Did you know that energy companies count their customers as their assets, not their energy?

They just buy energy and sell it to their customers.

It's the customers that are the assets.

And that is the brilliance of Company-Name.

It's a fantastic energy company that is offering energy to small business and consumers at a lower price than the old former monopolies were.

With those price, it's a no brainer for people to switch to Company-Name.

Company-Name saves money by not advertising, but by using word of mouth and word of mouse.

By allowing people like you and me to find their customers for them —
and reward us for doing it!

Network marketing.

When you join Company-Name and start building up your own customer
'asset' base — you earn income each and every month when the customer
pays the bill.

Each customer is an asset.

And Company-Name keeps on paying you because people don't stop using
electricity.

And if you take advantage of team building, you can help others create
assets as well.

And guess what? You get a share of their total billings too.

More assets.

More money.

It's a pretty simple concept.

Build up your asset portfolio for 'nothing down'.

Call me and I'll show you how to do this, it's not hard, and I'll
stick with you all the way.

Best,

Jane

contact info

online video

Lightning Forecast This Afternoon, Really

Hi Prospect-Name,

It's funny about money.

The way money works is just not fair.

The folks who feel they deserve it – usually those without it – don't acquire money easily.

But then again a lot of folks who work hard for it – also don't get it.

Gee.

I know everyone says you have to work smart.

Well, perhaps that's true.

Think about this from my buddy Earl:

Ben Franklin may have discovered electricity – but it is the man who invented the meter is who made the money.

That is sad, sad but true.

Now Franklin did pretty well with his money but he never many any cash from flying his kite in a lightning storm.

Along comes some guy who figures a way to sell it – and presto – MONEY!

Well, the money's in the marketing.

And that's why I'm marketing electricity.

There's money in it.

And there is even more money showing people how SAVE money each month by choosing smartly.

Here's our program: we show folks how they can save money each month on their energy bill and the energy company pays us a commission.

We show them one time and we get paid each month, month after month, year after year, for as long as they continue to use it…like forever!

And you don't have to be as smart Franklin to also see that this is network marketing.

Meaning if you recruit a team you'll get a further commission based on the usage of the customers signed on by your team.

You know, that is true residual income.

A lot of folks think that you need to sell a big-ticket item to make money in networking. Their reason is people don't stay with a company very long and stop buying autoship products.

Well sure. A lot of folks don't stay on autoship, but that's no reason to choose a big-priced product either.

Here at Company-Name we just offer products that people will buy with you or without you.

And with Company-Name, the price is less expensive than the existing utility.

And folks 'stay on the product'.

Nice.

So if you want to earn a bunch of Ben Franklins, a big bunch, don't wait for lightning to strike twice – pick up the phone and call me.

I'm here and ready to help you all the way.

Best,

Jane

contact info

online video

No One Wants to Change Diapers

Hello Prospect-Name,

Changing diapers is as much fun as herding chickens.

At least it's easier.

It's also easier than changing people's behavior.

Changing behavior is hard.

Like our belief on the type of car to own.

Here's what I mean, listen to what the founder of Paypal said about eCars"

Selling an electric sports car creates an opportunity to fundamentally change the way America drives. - Elon Musk

Now that is not a job I'd want. I was brought up with a gas-powered car and have a hard time thinking about any other kind.

But I can see the writing on the wall.

More and more eCars are on our highways and streets.

And I know a way we can make money as the spread of these silent little 'plugs' grows:

Selling energy.

That's why I got involved with Company-Name.

They sell energy, electricity. Power.

And they sell if for less.

Less is good - when it's the price.

I'll bet you can see the writing on the wall too.

I can help you get your own monthly paycheck based on energy customers too.

It makes sense - hey eCars are not science fiction - they are here.

So it's time to finally make some money from the work of Elon Musk - collect on his eCars - and all the other reasons people use electricity each and every day - by joining Company-Name.

Call me today, and I'll help you all the way,

Best,

Jane

contact info

online video

Mr. Spock Was Always Fascinated. But Was He Fascinating?

Hello Prospect-Name,

Spock was always saying 'fascinating' if you remember your Star Trek
lore. What to us was a mere Class-M planet was to him a 'fascinating
example of barbaric human tendencies'.

I wonder if Spock would have been fascinated by Oscar Wilde.

Wilde himself WAS fascinating.

See if this statement of Wilde's reminds you of anyone you know:

Anyone who lives within their means suffers from a lack of imagination.

Judging by the average household debt levels - a lot of us are not
suffering from a lack of imagination.

Now while no one would argue that Wilde was fascinating, he died in
Paris alone and penniless.

"It is better to have a permanent income than to be fascinating."

Wilde knew of what he spoke.

While many may wish to have the wit of Wilde, but no one wants to die
penniless.

The cure?

A permanent income.

How?

By building a business based on the monthly use of energy - something
that is permanent.

And you can do that with Company-Name.

Building a network of Company-Name energy marketers is not hard.

Most people who have had a taste of networking know how hard it is to convince people that their special product is, well, special.

And with the high price.

And sign up with an autoship plan.

With Company-Name everything is the other way around.

We save people money on something they already use, won't cancel, and will continue to buy.'

I'm not saying you'll end up like Wilde if you don't join us here at Company-Name – alone and penniless – but it's still good advice to get a permanent income.

If want a permanent income, call me. Call me today and I'll help you.

Best,

Jane

contact info

online video

Do You Know What is Really Attractive? Wink wink – It's Not What You Think

Hi Prospect-Name,

Richard Branson is a pretty handsome guy.

If you like that Robin Hood look.

But hey, there are no ugly billionaires.

He said something interesting about how to become a millionaire that I think we could agree is actually fool proof.

If you want to be a Millionaire, start with a billion dollars and launch a new airline.

Sadly, most of us are waiting for the business that gets us to the billion dollar part.

The bottom line is we want to earn some money.

It would be nice if money would come to us.

The secret: Dan Kennedy says, "Create a business that money is attracted to."

There is a lot of wisdom there.

Energy attracts.

It attracts money.

Each month people pay their energy bills, (the few who don't soon find out why that's not a good plan).

It's just the way it is: energy attracts money.

So how can you get in the way of that money flow?

Simple: with Company-Name.

Company-Name markets energy at a price point lower than what consumers and business are paying today.

People MUST pay that bill, yet are not averse to having it lowered.

They WANT to know about lower energy costs.

That's how we get paid.

We offer them lower energy costs, they like that and switch to Company-Name.

You can check out our prices yourself.

But more importantly, you can build a team of reps that will offer those savings on to others, and Company-Name will pay you a commission on that energy too.

Are you getting it? Energy attracts money, and you are in a business that money is attracted to.

Ready to start?

Call me now and I'll help you every step of the way.

Best,

Prospect-Name

contact info

online video

George Carlin and the Gold Mine

Hi Prospect-Name,

You may remember a comedian from the old school who was a pretty funny guy - name of George Carlin.

Here was something he said:

In America, anyone can become president. That's the problem.

But my favorite line of George's was…

Electricity is really just organized lightning.

Why do I like that? I guess because I'm in the energy game.

And I do pretty well in it.

Because I'm organized and I can find customers as fast as lightning.

How?

Well, this is what I say to them:

I don't know if I can help you or not, but if you'll give me a copy of last month's utility bills, I know a company that will analyze them for free to see if you're being overcharged.

People love to save money, and they like that you can give them a free 'energy price audit'.

It's cool.

That's why it's simple to get folks to switch over to Company-Name. And you know what? Company-Name pays a percentage of that bill to you.

It's a team effort as well.

If you are a team player and like to work with others, you can build a team and earn a percentage from their customers also.

Real residual income – except you do it as much or as little as you want – but keep getting paid on and on and on…and on.

Call me and I'll walk you through it.

Best,

Jane

contact info

online video

Post Scripts - PS's

Add a different PS to each of your emails. Repeat them as needed.

You can put the PS right after your contact info.

P.S.: How does the idea of making money on commercial energy sound to you?

P.S.: Our product is a public utility that is unconsciously purchased & habitually used… who says you need to be a sales type in network?

P.S.: How does the idea of making money on commercial energy sound to you?

P.S.: "I don't know if I can help you or not, but if you'll give me a copy of last month's utility bills, I'll have them analyzed for free to see if you're being overcharged". Could you say that? Of course you could!

P.S.: There's no cost to switch.

P.S.: Everybody understands the benefits of electricity - they have used it since birth!

P.S.: Our customers spend less.

P.S.: You don't have to convince somebody that they need electricity or natural gas. If you don't have it you want it really, really bad!

P.S.: Our customers love saving money!

P.S.: Nothing changes for the consumer!

P.S.: There's no merchandise to sell or deliver and no money to collect.

P.S.: We don't change the way the consumer buys the product.

P.S.: The business with no inventory to buy, product to deliver, or money to collect, and everyone already uses it.

P.S.: Everybody already understands our product! No more product demos! Nice!

P.S.: Why in the world would you get in a business where you've got to convince someone to buy something?

Further Resources

FREE! Five additional Email Autoresponders!!

Sign up for my newsletter and get five more generic email messages!

www.DavidWilliamsMLMAuthor.com

Books:

How to Recruit Doctors into your MLM or Network Marketing team by showing them a NO Warm Market System

http://www.amazon.com/Recruit-Doctors-Network-Marketing-ebook/dp/B00CCPZ7Z4

Where to Find Doctors - It's not where you think

A new source of Doctors (medical) who are not busy

Perfect for the Wellness Industry

No buying Leads

Not working the phone

This book is going to teach you an amazing system to recruit Doctors and an amazing system for you to build a huge, profitable and unstoppable leg under them - without the Doctor using any of their warm market, 'buying leads' or touching the phone!

Full Discloser: This is a short book. It's less than 50 pages long. It contains no fluff or padding. It's direct and to the point. The system contained is worth hundreds of thousands of dollars in sales, and could retire you. Really. Forget the low price of $8.99, forget the number of pages. This book will show you a fool proof system that ANY one can follow to build an unstoppable MLM Network Marketing business by recruiting Doctors. I have made it newbie friendly, but those with experience will take this system and put into practice very quickly.

This book will cover, step by step, and in very detailed and specific language:

The 'invisible' secret source of Doctors without a practice that are begging for something like what you will be able to show them

How to recruit busy Doctors with a practice and zero time

How to avoid the 'I don't want to go to my contacts/warm market' objection because you will be teaching them a system that requires ZERO warm market

And No 'buying leads'!

How to fill, yes FILL, meeting rooms with prospects all eager to join and try your products

NO conference calls, webinars, websites, Fanpages, autoresponders etc.

This is the full system, from the free ads you will place to the words on the marketing material you will print. This approached is very inexpensive to follow, quick and easy to implement, and very straight forward.

Also included are the phone scripts and person to person scripts you need to use when speaking to the Doctors, their receptionists, and to use in getting the appointment.

Forget all the 'usual suspects' techniques, this is not about dropping off DVDs, inviting them to conference calls, or creating special 'Doctors only' presentations. Forget all of that, and forget all of your old scripts and ads.

This system works for Doctors and requires NO Warm Market - I know I said that above, but it's very important you know this.

You don't need any paid advertising, Facebook, Internet, Twitter etc., this is all offline, local, and affordable.

No one has taught you this before. Guaranteed.

MLM Script Treasury: Not Your Usual Network Marketing Phone Scripts

http://www.amazon.com/Treasury-Network-Marketing-Scripts-ebook/dp/B00CKC5F38

By David Williams

This book is full of the top pulling, most valuable and very rare MLM phone scripts that have earned their users many hundreds of thousands of dollars. I will say right now, the material in this book is NOT 'newbie' friendly. These scripts are for pros. If you don't know what you're doing this book is not for you.

-Turn your prospects voice mail into a recruiting machine! 12 scripts which you can customize

-What do I say to make sure my prospects watch's my DVD or online presentation?

-What is a GAP line and why you should use one, and what to say on it.

-How to take your prospects pulse

-Top Tier Phone scripts – rare and valuable – and great to modify for your own phone scripts

-What to say to get your prospect on to a conference call

-How to close your prospect after a conference call – lots of trial closes, hard closes, and objection handlers

-Common objections and how to turn them back into closing questions

I have chosen scripts that I know you will NOT find in other script books for sale, or the free PDFs that float all over the Internet. The scripts contained here are the kind of scripts that only the top leaders in a program have access to and it usually requires someone to be invited to join their inner team to gain access to them.

This book is full of very hard hitting powerful scripts that have been used by many top prospectors and closers. You can use this book to build your own scripts by modifying what you find here.

-Scripts to get a prospect to commit to a live conference call

-The hardest closing questions from the industry

-Ads that will get your Voice Mail full, and what to say on your Voice Mail screener - lots of screeners and out bound messages

-What to say to your prospect AFTER the conference call

-Voice Scripts to 'wake up the dead' - get your inactive distributors active again

-Starting your own MLM or Team Call? Need a conference call script? - 4 full conference call scripts inside

-Are you a company trainer? Do you do many trainings? Are your people dying on the phone?

If you are a trainer, a serious upline, on your way to being a player, a 'big dog', this book is for you. If you are putting together your own scripts, calls, establishing your own team, or your own network marketing company - invest in this book. Inside this book you will find: hard hitting, hard closing power calls, what to say when you reach a prospects voice mail, screeners, actual company conference calls, GAP line messages and some special bonuses to get your phone ringing plus much, much more. It's all here.

What is in this book can take a serious player to the next level.

This is most definitely an 'insider's book'.

MLM Autoresponder Messages and Network Marketing Email Messages: Financial Woes Pack

http://www.amazon.com/Autoresponder-Messages-Network-Marketing-ebook/dp/B00D38WD38

This book contains a professionally written email drip campaign of 30 powerful, engaging and entertaining persuasive email/autoresponder messages focused on your prospects 'Financial Woes' and how YOU can help your prospect solve them.

Warning!

If you have been in Network Marketing for any length of time, you probably have accumulated a list of prospects and their email address. However, many of these prospects have entered the 'witness protection program'. In other words, they never call back or reply to your emails. Most people forget about this list, but there is GOLD in it!

Now, you probably have an email system you pay for that is filled with 'canned' autoresponders about your company, or even some generic versions to send to your list. Sometimes this is part of your 'backoffice'.

But, have you read these autoresponders being sent in your name?

They suck.

Here's why:

You have a prospect who is looking to solve THEIR problem, which is lack of money. They need money, income, some light at the end of the tunnel, cash, maybe some dough to save their home... BUT they are NOT shopping for a MLM company, an INDUSTRY, or how long your company has been in business, or even what your product does…NO… they are desperate for a SOLUTION to their problems!

But if all the emails you send out are about 'the company, the timing, the industry…or how someone else is making money – no wonder they don't bother responding to you!

Can you imagine sending emails to starving children with stories about the kids in your family that have so much food… that they're fat? Of course not. So why send emails to financially struggling people about how others are rich?

Your prospect doesn't care about other people's wealth when THEY are broke and in financial pain. In fact, it works the other why. Resentment, suspicion, distrust.

Their mind is on their lack of money and they are worried.

They are awake all night worrying about their debt because they are in financial trouble.

And what? You send them an email about how old your company is?

It's basic marketing folks; offer your prospect a solution to their problem, and relate to them on their terms.

At this point, all your prospect is interested in is finding 'a way to earn money'.

NOTE *** If you are new and have not earned a respectable income, chances are your upline will tell you to borrow someone else's story, but doing that only begs the question from your prospect- 'well, if everyone else is making money in your company, why aren't you?'

Forget that.

So, what is in this book? Do I teach you how to write emails? NO…NO…and NO!!!!

Is this some lessons on basic copy writing for MLM? Heck NO!!!

But let's face it. Most people can't write a note to save their lives, let alone a well-crafted email campaign. Forget learning a skill that will take you years to master - just use expert messages instead!

That's where this book of powerful 'financial woes' autoresponder messages will come to your aid.

Inside are 30 rock solid emails that focus on your prospects financial situation - with engaging humor and playfulness - showing how YOU and your program can help him out of his or her financial mess.

FULL DISCLOUSER - this is a small book - 30 powerful emails. You are not paying for the quantity of words, you are paying for the quality of the message and for getting your phone to ring.

This book contains 30 well-crafted powerfully written emails that and fun and engaging that will suggest and reinforce to your prospect that YOU are the answer to their financial problems using proven psychological and persuasion techniques.

Take these email autoresponder messages and enter them into your backoffice or your email program. Start dripping on your list with these professionally written email messages – each crafted to have your prospect motivated to reach out and call YOU as an answer to their Financial Woes!

How to Prospect and Recruit using Postcards for your MLM or Network Marketing Business The Low cost Prospecting and Recruiting Tool that Out Performs Online Methods

http://www.amazon.com/Postcards-Marketing-Prospecting-Recruiting-ebook/dp/B00EVZG8R4

Fed up not having quality leads?

Are you in a MLM company you love, but just can't find REAL prospects to talk to?

Tried 'online' leads but found you just wasted your time and money?

Many networkers are well past the 'warm market' stage, and are struggling to find success. It seems the entire world has gone online and the problem that networkers face is sticking out in an ever increasing ocean of websites, mobile apps, opt-in forms, blog posts, Facebook Likes, Youtube movies and Tweets. It never ends.

There is alternative. There is another way.

Because the world HAS gone online, good old fashioned Direct Mail is making a comeback. Why? Because no one gets 'real' mail anymore. You have zero competition!

And what's more real than a picture postcard?

NOTE:

What This Book is NOT about: this book in no way teaches you to send those ugly, tacky, pre-printed, glossy pictures of fast expensive cars or mansions, or YELLOW 'print your own' postcards. NO, NO, NO!

If you are engaged in postcard marketing, buying glossy tacky 'in your face' MLM style postcards and mailing them out - or worse - paying to have them mailed out - I'll show you a method that will increase your success by a massive amount - because I guarantee your message will be read if you use the method I teach.

Or, if you are prospecting with one of those 'print your own' cards at the local Office Max, mailing out thousands until you're broke by sending ugly cards - you will be so happy switching to my method because it will save you time, money, you'll mail out less cards and get massive more results.

Again, because I guarantee your prospect will read your message.

I will show you a method that combines two of the most important recruiting factors for success in MLM:

Mass Recruiting and Personalization

And NO - this is not about using computer 'hand writing fonts'!!!

I'll show you a method to recruit massively with postcards, in a very personal-ized way for your prospect to find it impossible to not read your message and make a call.

This works. This book is based on my famous postcard seminars that were part of a $10,000 MLM insider's weekend training. You will get this same information for less than $10. And the best part of it is, this system works even better today than before! Why? Because the power of a postcard, personalized, is stronger today in this Internet age.

Full Disclosure: This is a short, to the point book. It's not full of padding or fluff, (however, I do trace for you how I discovered my introduction into Direct Mail for MLM Recruiting by a presidential fundraiser).

It's a 'How To' book. You are paying for the system, the magic, and the fact that you won't need any other information to get started.

I have included low or no budget methods as well.

Please NOTE: This book is for MLM or Network Marketing recruiting - it's not about postcard 'marketing' for non-MLM business. The information here is for network marketers who want to build downlines and offer a system to their team that does not rely on 'buying leads' from the internet and telemarketing 'survey leads', 'real time leads', 'fresh leads', or any of the other scammy descrip-tions of absolutely terrible leads for sale by lead companies.

Looking for a Low cost, but highly efficient network marketing tool way to get REAL leads? This is it.

Forget Internet leads - recruit real people, not virtual names.

How to Prospect and Recruit using Postcards for your MLM or Network Marketing Business - The Low cost Prospecting and Recruiting Tool that Out Performs Online Methods is a complete method. Includes the way to personalize the cards, where to buy them at the best prices, how to produce them, where to get the lists to mail your cards to, as well as how to do this on a low or no budget.

You will also get a '24 hour' message to load up on your voice mail system to take all the calls you'll get from your prospects.

How to create the personalized card

Where to get your cards wholesale

What to say on the card

Where to get lists and how to deal with list brokers

Low and no budget tricks and strategies

Text for your 24 hour message your prospects calls after reading your card

If you have run out of ways of recruiting, if your upline is no help, take action yourself and invest in your business by using this book on how to recruit and build a team with postcards.

This system works in USA, Canada and Europe - I know because I have used it in each of those countries and built huge downlines in this way.

The Simplest, Shortest, Most Powerful MLM and Network Marketing Prospect Control and Closing Lines and Scripts

http://www.amazon.com/Network-Marketing-Online-Professional-ebook/dp/B00DVCTK78

Do you have trouble closing prospects? Do you feel you lose control of your prospecting and follow up calls? Do you have trouble closing strong prospects – the very ones you desperately want on your team?

Well, this book is for you. It's the lowest price but highest value book on Amazon. Why? Because this little book contains over 120 of the strongest, easiest, subtlest closing and 'keeping control' and 'taking control' over the conversation lines for network marketers.

FULL DISCLOSURE: This is a short book. This book has over 150 'lines'; mostly one line sentences. But don't be fooled by the size of the book. These are powerful closing lines to allow you to close your prospect. This is NOT a book on prospecting, recruiting or even a script book.

This is a book that should be open at your desk as you make your prospecting and follow up calls. If you find you prospect off their script (they never stay on script – only you can do that), these lines will bring you back into control.

They are subtle, but powerful. Here's some samples:

How much does it cost?

Millions of dollars not to get involved

Can you see yourself taking people through a process just like I did with you?

You can't outsource your learning

The table's set

This is thick

I'm not claiming we have an automatic system, I'm demonstrating it

Get into the game with us

Let me layout how the business will start for you

This is just a process to see if there a fit for you

This is not a pressure gig

It's just the way we do this (process)

There's no glory in paying bills

I promise I'm not going to push you, chase you or sell you

I'm not going to come back to close you, but to personalize the business for you

NOTE: with very little modification, you can use many of these lines as ad headers, email subject lines, or as smart and directed text in emails or create new phone scripts or reinvigorate old ones.

Now, you don't have to memorize these lines, you just need to have your Kindle reader, iPad or even your Kindle for PC open, (or you can print out the pages), when you are making your calls. If you lose control of a conversation, or have a strong person on the line (the best kind to recruit), these 'lines' are the arrows in your quiver.

Make these lines your own. They have been collected by professionals and have earned those who have used them millions of dollars, no exaggerating, millions of dollars. Now for .99 cents they are yours.

This book of powerful network marketing closing and control lines provides you with the easiest way to sound strong on the phone. You just need to use them. You need to sound strong. Your prospect will never know what hit them until you are training them, and tell them to pick up this little book.

If they won't spend .99 cents, to get a copy, they aren't worth your time. If they ask you to make them a copy instead, they have just told you they are not worth your time. You now own this book, make these lines your own, become powerful and rich.

You do deserve it!

About the Author

If you want to remember one thing about David Williams it's this:

He believes in OFFLINE prospecting and ONLINE follow up!

David Williams has been a top earner and top performer in networking for over 25 years. He has worked all over the world building teams successfully. In the last five years he has worked with corporations to develop MLM opportunities as well as top performers to create recruiting systems for their teams.

He also delivers 'insider only' high priced seminars for 'the big dogs' on practical MLM: prospecting, recruiting and team expansion.

Prior to Networking Williams' background was psychology and organization building.

In 2012 he decided to put into book-form some of the trainings he has done, and offer them on Amazon. He does not do any marketing for these books. There is one part-time staff member at his very small publishing house that does promote his work. Typically his work spreads word-of-mouth and word-of-mouse. Williams decided to present his insiders training at price levels that are affordable via Amazon to anyone but is not trying to disrupt the high priced seminars business either. Rather he feels that his readers are new and future leaders who are not even aware of these insider events but will one day will be seated there if they follow his systems.

Williams is not actively working any MLM program but enjoys 8 different residual income sources and in multiple currencies.

His favorite MLM tips include:

- Fire your Upline
- Be the Upline you want
- Never stop recruiting
- How much money would I make today if my downline did what I did?

He hates 'fluff' training.

He writes a MLM email training letter that he sends weekly - you can sign up too at www.DavidWilliamsMLMAuthor.com

Those who have signed up for David's newsletter my reach him via that email address. Feel free to contact him with any question.

Made in the USA
Middletown, DE
15 October 2018